TIMPSON
ON THE
VERGE

❖

Norfolk village signs
investigated by

John Timpson

Photographs by John Bacon

Additional photographs by
Nicolette Hallett

Larks Press

Published by the Larks Press
Ordnance Farmhouse, Guist Bottom,
Dereham, Norfolk NR20 5PF

Tel/Fax:01328 829207
E-mail: larkspress@talk21.com

Printed by the Lanceni Press
Garrood Drive, Fakenham

May 2000

British Library Cataloguing-in-Publication Data
A catalogue record for this book is available from the British Library

ISBN 0 948400 89 7

NORFOLK'S ROADSIDE GALLERY

Norfolk may be famous for its profusion of medieval churches, but it has nearly as many illustrated village signs – and with so many parishes erecting new ones to mark the Millennium, the signs are catching up fast. There are now about five hundred of them, more than in any other county in Britain, a roadside gallery of local legends, characters and events, providing a unique guide to what are often the quirkier aspects of Norfolk's rural history.

Some signs date back to the early years of the twentieth century, when the royal family introduced the idea on the Sandringham estate, but the main surge came during the nineteen-fifties, prompted by the Queen's Coronation. Parishes wanted their own permanent and individual reminder of the occasion. It continued into the 'sixties and 'seventies, when there were other events and anniversaries to celebrate, from the Silver Jubilee to the fiftieth anniversary of the Norfolk Federation of Women's Institutes. The WIs in fact have been among the principal donors of village signs, as their initials on so many of them testify.

Throughout this period, one man's name constantly recurred. Harry Carter, the art and woodwork master at Hamond's Grammar School in Swaffham, designed and carved his first sign for his home town before the second World War, and when he died in 1983 there were over 150 Harry Carter signs in towns and villages throughout Norfolk, with another seventy-odd in neighbouring counties. Whenever a parish council or a local organisation wanted to mark a special occasion, like the Old Testament prophets the cry went up: 'Give us a sign, Harry!' And Harry did – often quite literally, charging only for his materials.

As the years went on, some of the signs had to be replaced, often by metal or even plastic replicas, and others were lost altogether. But more artists and designers came along, and more signs were erected, culminating in the current increase in enthusiasm over the Millennium.

This book contains a selection of the most intriguing and ingenious ones, covering the length and breadth of Norfolk, from King John with his treasure at Walpole Cross Keys in the west to the eight-oared lifeboat at Sea Palling in the east, and from Thornham's unlikely iron foundry in the north to the T-shaped town sign at Diss in the south, with the royal tutor John Skelton on one side, and on the other a victim of royalty, Matilda Fitzwalter, who rebuffed King John and subsequently died from a poisoned egg.

There are signs from as far back as the 'wolf' signpost at Wolferton, which bears the date 1912, to very new ones marking the Millennium. The most recent of these, as I write, was only officially unveiled at Hockering this April. It is in traditional style, featuring the parish church and the River Tudd, a deer to represent all those that used to graze in Hockering Wood, and lilies-of-the-valley and bluebells, which still grow there in profusion.

The drawing of the Ingham sign is a foretaste of those planned for later this year. Among its other features it shows a swan with the ownership mark of the sixteenth-century Lord of the Manor on its beak, and from more recent times a bat and ball to represent the local cricket club. It is the work of an Ingham art teacher, Joe Blossom; I am sure Harry Carter, another art teacher, would approve...

Nearly all the photographs in this book were taken by John Bacon, a wartime Royal Marine Commando and later works foreman in Doncaster, who came to Norfolk in 1996, after his wife died, in order to be near his daughter's home in Wymondham. His interest in photography led to his retirement hobby of photographing Norfolk signs, and in the next three years he accumulated a collection of more than 450. He was still photographing Millennium signs when he was taken ill suddenly and died just before Christmas 1999, aged 78.

John Bacon never saw his work published, but I hope this book provides a fitting memorial to a great enthusiast for rural Norfolk.

John Timpson

ALDBOROUGH

Aldborough might well have been overshadowed by its Suffolk near-namesake when Benjamin Britten and his friends began their famous concerts, but the Norfolk village is just as renowned locally for its Fair as Aldeburgh is for its Festival. It has been held for over 700 years, since King John presented the original charter for an annual livestock fair. It was also a hiring fair for servants and labourers. These days you can't acquire a few sheep or a couple of kitchen-maids, but if you are lucky you may still win a goldfish or a cuddly toy.

One side of the sign depicts a traditional scene at the fair, before the advent of shooting galleries and dodg'ems. The other side shows men working in a tannery, from the days when Aldborough had two of them, plus two saddlers, a whip-maker, a smithy and many more. The sign nestles cosily under a little thatched roof – though, ironically, thatching was one of the few rural trades not listed in the village records.

1

ALDEBY

Aldeby's elegant wooden sign started life in a very different role. The wood came from an old level-crossing gate in the village dating back to pre-Beeching days. The longboat it depicts harks back to a much earlier form of transport, when the Vikings sailed up the river to colonise the area.

However, not everyone agrees about the village's origins. The pro-Viking lobby argues that the 'by' in Aldeby was Scandinavian for 'farm', but others say the name was spelt 'Aldeburgh' in Domesday Book and thus is Anglo-Saxon. Now a new book on Norfolk place-names (published, happily, by the Larks Press!) very fairly points out that Old Norse and Anglo-Saxon had the same Germanic roots, and over the years they merged very easily, so Aldeby could be either. But the book does come down in favour of the Vikings, so the longboat now sails unchallenged on its curly ornamental waves.

The other features on the sign are entirely uncontroversial: a sheaf of corn representing farming, and a bunch of apples denoting the local apple orchards and the Waveney Apple Growers' 'apple factory', a major seasonal employer.

ANMER

It may seem odd for a tiny village of some thirty dwellings to be defended, on its village sign, by a Roman soldier and a Boy Scout, back to back under the royal coat of arms. It may also seem odd that a village this size has not only a church, a Methodist chapel and a stately home, but also a cosy village hall and a clubhouse with its own bowling green.

But Anmer is on the Sandringham royal estate. Most of the cottages used to be occupied by estate workers, Anmer Hall was the home of the Duke and Duchess of Kent, and royal shoots still take place nearby. So the royal family takes a special interest in the village and its amenities. The village hall, for instance, was given by King George V and Queen Mary, and the altar cloth in the parish church was also donated by Queen Mary.

As for the Scout and the Roman soldier, legend has it that the Romans fought Queen Boadicea not far away, hence the soldier, and many centuries later the Scouts held a jamboree at Anmer Park. They then donated the sign as a thank-you to the Queen, as well as a permanent reminder of their visit.

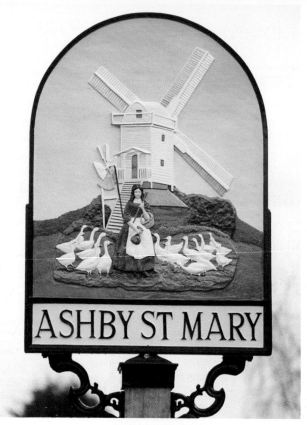

ASHBY ST MARY

In 1868 an illustrated tombstone was erected in the churchyard to a local farmer's wife, Ann Basey, depicting her feeding her geese in the farmyard. In March 2000 a village sign was erected to mark the Millennium, and again Ann Basey features on it, but this time in her earlier years, when she had a much more energetic role. As well as just fattening up the geese, she finished the job by driving them on foot down to London each year for the Michaelmas sales.

It was a long, hard walk, as tough on the geese as it was on her, and to prevent the birds getting sore feet she coated their soles with tar to harden them up. During the journey the geese literally lived off the land, eating the grain left behind in the fields of corn stubble. It was no doubt small consolation to them that, unlike Ann Basey, they did not have to walk all the way back.

The sign also shows Ashby's old postmill, which was working until the early nineteen hundreds. Then its sails were damaged in a gale and it was pulled down a few years later.

ASHMANHAUGH

This sign poses something of a riddle. How does a bishop on a river bank, surmounted by a tree, represent Ashmanhaugh? The answer, like most answers when you know them, is very simple. Split the name into Ash-man-haugh. The ash is the tree on the top of the sign and the man is St Swithin, patron saint of the parish church. The *haugh* is not quite so obvious, unless you speak fluent Anglo-Saxon. It comes from *haga*, meaning an enclosure of land and stream, and there indeed is the land and the stream, with the parish church included for good measure .Incidentally it would have been interesting to stick to Anglo-Saxon origins for 'Ashman' too. It comes from *aesomann*, which means not a bishop but a pirate...

The two coats of arms are those of St Swithin and the Prestons, who used to be the local landowners. The church tower may look quite lofty in the painting, but it is actually the lowest round tower in Norfolk.

BAWBURGH

The legend of St Walstan was only put on paper three or four centuries after his death in 1019, so experts are a little sceptical about the details, but he still rates top billing on Bawburgh's sign.

Walstan was said to be a Saxon nobleman's son, who gave up everything to labour in the fields atTaverham, living a humble life and being generally saintly. On his deathbed the priest administering the last rites found he had no water to mix with the wine, whereupon Walstan said a prayer and a holy spring appeared.He asked for his body to be hauled away on a cart drawn by two white oxen (also featured on the sign) and buried wherever they stopped. They finished up at Bawburgh, he was duly buried, and another holy spring appeared nearby. His shrine was a place of pilgrimage until the Reformation, and the locals made a useful income from selling the holy water on Norwich market. The water is no longer drinkable, but there is still an annual service and procession in honour of St Walstan, followed by a picnic - and they say it never rains until lunch is safely over!

BEETLEY

The sign illustrates the village's name, as any early Anglo-Saxon could tell you, but to the visitor today the connection is not obvious. It shows a clearing in a wood with a young man banging a stake into the ground with a wooden mallet, rather like the ones used on fairground 'test-your-strength' machines. There are some pretty flowers and lots of grass, but not a sugar-beet or even a beetle in sight - or so it seems.

But in Anglo-Saxon times that mallet would have been called a *bettel* or *bietel,* and a woodland clearing was a *lea.* Put the two together, allow for a few adjustments over the centuries, and Bietel-lea becomes Beetley, a clearing where mallets were made.

With wooden posts forming the basis for most dwellings, as well as stockades to protect them, Beetley's mallets made from local trees must have been in great demand. The trees came in handy again a thousand years later, when a parapet was added to the church tower in 1911. The parapet is not made of wooden posts, but it was paid for - rather regrettably perhaps - by selling the oak trees in the churchyard.

BLAKENEY (SEE COVER)

Most of the features on Blakeney's sign have fairly obvious reasons for being there. The central galleon, for instance, recalls how the village sent three ships to face the Armada when it was a thriving seaport - before a thoughtless landowner built a bank across the River Glaven and caused the silt which now limits the channel to small holiday craft.

The mallard and tern above the ship represent the bird sanctuary at Blakeney Point, and the two dolphins underneath add a further maritime flavour. But how about the two hammers with a stone between them, and the gentleman with the fiddle eying the gloomy entrance to a tunnel?

As at Beetley, the hammers used to be known as bietels, and the 'stone' is in fact a chestnut. They illustrate the obscure and rather insulting local rhyme:

Blakeney people go up the steeple
To crack a small nut with a five-farthing bietel.

As for the fiddler, it is said that he vowed to follow a tunnel to Wiveton, fiddling all the way, a legend which crops up elsewhere in Norfolk. The fiddler vanished and so did the tunnel, but if you listen closely, somewhere down there the fiddle plays on...

BLOFIELD HEATH

The origin of the 'Blo' in Blofield Heath is open to debate. It could be the Old English word *blaw*, referring to the blue pigment which we know better as woad. But blaw has another meaning too, just 'bleak'. Either meaning could have applied to almost anywhere in Norfolk in Saxon times, so when Mrs Jill Ward of the local Women's Institute was planning a design for the village sign she wisely went for a straightforward pun on the present day word 'blow'. Hence the very bent tree, blowing in the wind. The other modern meaning of 'blow' is covered too, because the sign has been a big hit!

The rest of the design is straightforward enough. The 'field' in Blofield is just that, with a farmer working in it on his tractor, and the 'heath' is symbolised by a sprig of heather. The WI had the idea of the sign to commemorate the centenary of the movement in 1998, but it all took a little time, as these things do, and it was unveiled in the autumn of 1999 - in good time for the Millennium! Local craftsmen made and erected it on land belonging to the village pub.

BRADENHAM

East and West Bradenham are both represented by the emblems of their churches, but most of the sign is devoted to one man. The exception is the gibbet, which is just a reminder of the local Gallows Hill. But Henry Rider Haggard was born in the farmhouse, and the farming scenes around him reflect his interest in agriculture.

His father was squire at Bradenham Hall, but at the time of his birth the Hall was let and they were living at Wood Farm on the estate. His mother said that as he was born on a farm 'the land will hold him all his life', but at nineteen his father sent him off to South Africa, and for years the nearest he got to farming was trying to raise ostriches. He failed, but his writing prospered, and *King Solomon's Mines* made him famous.

He returned to his wife's family home, Ditchingham Hall, to run the estate and write more books. In 1918 Bradenham Hall was sold, probably cheaply because he noted rather bitterly, 'The remoter parts of Norfolk are no longer desirable as places of residence.' If he could only have hung on...

BRISLEY

The figure in the large cap and long robe has such a chilling expression he might be sentencing someone to be hanged, drawn and quartered, but he is in fact Richard Taverner, the Brisley boy who shone at Cambridge and Oxford, became a Protestant preacher and found favour with Cardinal Wolsey.

The large book in his lap is his revised version of the Bible. According to local legend he worked on it in premises at the rear of the Bell Inn, but he hardly looks the sort to join the lads afterwards in the bar. The Taverner Bible was published in the 1530s, but experts say it had little influence on sub-sequent translations. He be-came Clerk to the Privy Seal, a job he surprisingly managed to retain for nearly thirty years, even during the entire reign of the Catholic Queen Mary. Elizabeth made him Sheriff of Oxfordshire, where he died and was buried, but his father's memorial brass is in the nave of Brisley church, depicted behind him on the sign.

BURNHAM THORPE

Not so much a village sign, more an illustrated memorial. Indeed the whole village, from the parish church to the local pub, seems devoted to revering the memory of its most famous son, Admiral Lord Nelson.

Young Horatio was born in the former Rectory, was christened in the church, and in due course drank in the pub, now named after him. The church is full of his relics, the pub has a fair number too, and since 1975 there has been the village sign, emblazoned with his name and date of birth, his portrait flanked by the Union Jack and the White Ensign, and a list of some of the ships he commanded and the battles he won. The centrepiece is a picture of his birthplace, the now demolished Rectory.

I suppose something else must have happened in Burnham Thorpe during its long existence, apart from Nelson's birth, but there is no hint of it on the sign. This is Nelson country, and there is no way you can turn a blind eye.

BURSTON

Burston gained national fame in the pre-war years because of the Burston School Strike, the longest in English history. It started in 1914 after the dismissal of the two popular school-teachers, Tom and Kitty Higdon, who had fallen foul of the chairman of the school governors. The children walked out in protest, there was widespread support from trade unionists all over the country, and a strike fund raised enough money for the Higdons to build their own school on the village green. The Strike School flourished until Tom Higdon died in 1939, a quarter of a century later. It is now a museum.

Inevitably the sign commemorates the strike, but not very obviously. Its main feature is a sheaf of corn, framed by a horseshoe on a circular base, symbolising local agriculture But it is the post on which it stands that provides the link. It is carved with a barleytwist pattern, reminiscent of a vertical barber's pole, which actually represents a maypole, and the children of the village dance around it with their coloured ribbons every May Day in memory of their predecessors' fight for justice for their teachers.

CARBROOKE

The sign recalls a hardly-remembered episode in Norfolk's history, when the Knights Templar and later the Knights Hospitaller of St John of Jerusalem had a religious house at Carbrooke, the only one of its kind in the county.

The Templars were a religious military order dedicated to protecting pilgrims to the Holy Land, and the Hospitallers provided lodgings and hospitality. In the twelfth century Roger de Clare founded a small Commandery for the Templars at Carbrooke. It seems a long way from Jerusalem, but it was considered a Good Thing to Do.

Roger's widow Maud has been given the credit for passing it on to the Hospitallers, but in fact the Templars were suppressed in 1312, largely through jealousy of their wealth, and much of their property went to the Hospitallers anyway. In England they too were later suppressed for much the same reason, this time by Henry VIII, and that was the end of the Carbrooke Commandery - until the village sign.

Today the St John Ambulance Service preserves the Hospitallers' white cross on a black background, and the Templars' red cross is used by - yes, the Red Cross.

CARLETON FOREHOE

I always like to picture Carleton Forehoe as the name of a dashing young hero in a Restoration comedy, or perhaps a rakish fox in a children's storybook, watching nonchalantly from behind a tree as the hunt goes galloping by. But in reality Carleton means, in both Old English and Old Norse, an enclosure or settlement for free peasants, and Forehoe means four mounds. So the 'free peasants' are shown having a mardle on the best-known feature of the village to road-users, the hump-backed bridge over the River Tiffey. It was built in 1815 for the Wodehouses of Kimberley Hall, and the river feeds the lake at the Hall. The whole area, in fact, was part of the estate owned by the Wodehouse family for over five centuries, until it was sold in 1958.

Also on the sign are the 'Forehoe' or four mounds, a reminder of a group of tumuli on the village outskirts. The other half of the sign is devoted to the parish church as the spiritual hub of this little hamlet.

There are only about fifty people in Carleton Forehoe, but they were determined to have a village sign for the Millennium. The design was a corporate village project, and it was completed not only on time but with £15 to spare.

CASTLE ACRE

There was the choice of two famous old buildings to feature on Castle Acre's sign, the Norman castle and the Cluniac priory. One was built by the Conqueror's son-in-law, William de Warenne, the other by de Warenne's son. But the castle has long since been reduced to the remains of its keep and its curtain wall, whereas the lofty west front of the priory still stands, along with the prior's house and other substantial remains. It is reckoned to be the finest monastic ruin in East Anglia.

So it is not surprising that the sign is entirely devoted to the priory, restored to its original glory, with a chubby-cheeked monk standing beneath it, looking rather smug.

In the last century Castle Acre had plenty of other activities, including two corn mills, two smithies, an assortment of other small industries, and even a theatre, situated appropriately in Drury Lane. Since then the village population has halved, but thanks to its attractive village centre, and of course its handsome sign, the summer tourists easily make up its original numbers.

CAWSTON

This is one of Harry Carter's earlier and more elaborate signs, marking George VI's coronation. The centrepiece represents the former local weaving industry, and three of the smaller panels represent farming, the Royal Manor dating back to King Harold, and St Agnes, the church's patron saint. But I find the fourth panel most fascinating. The urn on a pedestal is known as the Duel Stone. It stands just outside the village as a reminder of a fatal sword-fight three centuries ago between two local squires.

Sir Henry Hobart of Blickling Hall was told that his near neighbour and political opponent, Oliver Le Neve, had called him a coward, and he forthwith challenged him to a duel. Le Neve denied ever saying it, but Sir Henry forced the issue by publicly insulting him, which of course no gentleman could tolerate. When they met on Cawston Heath, Sir Henry drew blood first, wounding Le Neve in the right arm, but fortunately for Le Neve he was left-handed, and was still able to inflict a mortal body-wound on Sir Henry. Le Neve had to flee the country, but later returned to face trial and was acquitted. So he lived to fight anotherday – but wisely didn't.

14

CHEDGRAVE

The story behind Chedgrave's sign is summed up in three words on the memorial plaque to David Clark, a retired deputy headmaster of nearby Langley School who was parish council chairman for ten years. It says simply: 'His ambition fulfilled'. He had always wanted a village sign, but various problems had arisen, and it was not until after his death in 1988 that it finally materialised – as a sign of remembrance.

It was made by a fellow schoolmaster, Jack Barwick, to a specific brief. It should be three-dimensional, using a plain natural material, and it should incorporate the oldest part of the oldest building in the parish. The result is a four-sided wooden sign surmounted by a replica of the Norman church tower, complete with little lead roof, and the edges of the sign are inscribed with the various spellings of the village's name. It derives from the Old English *Ceatta graf* or *graef,* but the Danish villager who was consulted by the compilers of Domesday Book mispronounced it and it went down as 'Scatagrava'. A century later it was corrected to 'Chattagrava', and eventually 'Chatta' became 'Ched'. It was not necessarily Ceatta's grave; the alternative meaning is just a grove.

COSTESSEY

Costessey could well have featured St Walstan on the sign, because in Costessey Woods there is St Walstan's Well where the two oxen hauling his bier from Taverham to Bawburgh decided to take a rest. But the saint appears on both those village signs, so Costessey wisely concentrates on its other claim to historical fame, the rise and fall of Costessey Hall.

The original Tudor mansion was built by Sir Henry Jerningham after being granted the Manor by Queen Mary. The staunchly Catholic family suffered during the Civil War, but remained at the Hall. Then a new kind of problem arose after Sir George Jerningham married into the Earl of Stafford's family and in due course the Jerninghams acquired the barony.

The first Jerningham baroness was very forceful – or bostessey as they might say in Costessey. She persuaded her husband to enlarge the Hall on such a grandiose scale in the nineteenth century that he never managed to complete it. The half-finished pile was put up for sale, but nobody wanted it and a demolition contractor knocked most of it down. The ruins are now on a golf course; non-golfers might call it the final ignominy...

The knotted piece of rope at the top recalls a story of three men on the Staffords' estate who were due to be hanged. They were promised a reprieve if they devised a knot which could be used to hang all three at once. They produced this 'Staffordshire Knot', and I hope they got their reprieve – or did the Lord of the Manor say he would have to test the knot on them first?

DENVER

Denver has a history as long as most Norfolk villages, with a church dating from the thirteenth century and a manor house going back to the Tudors. It also has a famous son, Captain George Manby, who went to school with Nelson (so tradition says) and later invented a rocket-fired lifeline which has saved as many lives at sea as were lost in all Nelson's battles.

But the village sign features quite different subjects. On one side is Denver's splendid old windmill, now being restored by the Norfolk Historic Buildings Trust with much local help, and on the other is Denver Sluice, the massive structure a mile outside the village which controls the water flow in and out of the Fens.

The Women's Institute, in its village survey, makes only a brief reference to these landmarks. It dwells more on the benefit of the A10 bypass and the complications caused by the Downham Market relief road, which slices off part of the village. But for most visitors it is the windmill and the sluice that make Denver memorable, and this has obviously been recognised by the W.I. because it has put them on the sign.

17

DILHAM

The sign is a reminder of a modest canal-building project, which never achieved great success but managed to survive for over a century until it finally succumbed in 1934. The North Walsham and Dilham Canal was opened in 1826, but it could only take three wherries a day and the competition from roads and railways was finally too much for it - and indeed for the wherries as well. Now only a short section is still usable by small holiday craft, though some would like to see it reopened, while others want it preserved as a nature reserve.

A canal bridge and a wherry are the main features on the sign, with reminders of two other defunct local industries, a windmill and a pair of brick kilns. On the post is carved the outline of a dill plant, the aromatic herb which grew so extensively in the area that it put the Saxon *dile* in Dilham.

This was the birthplace of Sir William Cubitt, a miller's son who became a famous civil engineer. He constructed docks, railways and drainage systems all over the country, and in 1851 he was knighted for his work on the Great Exhibition. So far as I know, he wisely had no connection with the North Walsham & Dilham Canal.

DISS

Like other town signs designed by Harry Carter the one at Diss is T-shaped. This T-for-town had the advantage of giving him two tall panels to work on for his main subjects, and he makes full use of them here.

On one side is the Revd John Skelton, local Rector, Poet Laureate, and tutor to Henry VII's children, including the future Henry VIII. He is shown teaching his royal charges. As Poet Laureate he once wrote a verse about his own verses:

> *Though my rime be ragged,*
> *Tattered and jagged,*
> *It hath in it some pith.'*

You can't get much pithier than that!

On the other panel is another local resident who was rather too popular with royalty. Matilda Fitzwalter, daughter of the Lord of the Manor, took the fancy of King John, but unwisely rejected his amorous advances. He forthwith disposed of her with a poisoned poached egg. Which confirms that not only was King John a bounder, but there's no such thing as a free breakfast.

Elsewhere on the sign a shield with wavy blue lines represents Diss Mere, and the decorations on the base show weaving, farming, and a seventeenth-century Diss farthing. The panels, I think, are much more fun.

DOWNHAM MARKET

Half-a-dozen different aspects of Downham Market are represented on its town sign. Even the brick base is part of its history; the bricks came from the stableyard of the old workhouse.

The two white horses on top of the sign are reminders of the horse fair which used to be held there, and the shield is St Edmund's, patron saint of the parish church. In the spandrels are a churn to represent the local butter-making industry, and the initials of the Women's Institute, which presented the sign.

One side of the upright shows St Winnold, a local sixth-century saint, ringing a handbell like a schoolteacher summoning his pupils, but according to legend he used the bell to call in the fish at feeding time, and sure enough the hungry fish are there too, popping out of the water.

On the other side is a young Nelson who attended the grammar school for a time. He holds a toy boat, hinting at his future triumphs, and behind him is a shadowy figure, which has been mistaken for a teacher, but it actually symbolises womanhood - no connection with a certain Lady Hamilton, I am assured, more likely a discreet reminder of who presented the sign.

EAST DEREHAM

The story of St Withburga, and how it put the 'Dere' into East Dereham, is one of the best-known tales in Norfolk's history, and the town sign depicts a scene from it in a most dramatic way. It stretches right across the High Street, a lofty tableau that seems to be running on wheels, like a low-loader truck crossing a bridge. But the wheels are just the emblem of Dereham Rotary Club, which donated Harry Carter's impressive sign on the town's 1300th anniversary.

It depicts an unfriendly bailiff and his dog hunting the two does which provided milk for the saint and her handmaidens while their nunnery was being built. Withburga is watching, looking quite calm in the circumstances. Perhaps she already knew the rest of the story – before the reeve could catch the deer he was thrown by his horse and broke his neck.

When Withburga died she was buried in the churchyard, until many years later a covetous Abbot of Ely, noting all the pilgrims that came to her grave, sent his monks by night to steal her body. But Dereham had the last laugh. A holy well appeared on the site of the grave, attracting more pilgrims than ever.

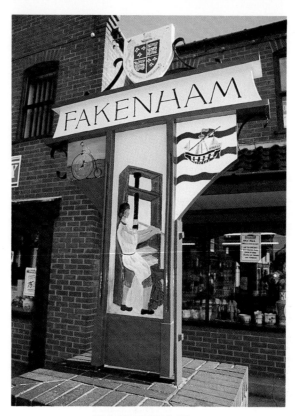

FAKENHAM

To get the point of all the symbols on this elaborate sign you need to delve deep into Fakenham's history - or, more simply, read the plaque provided by Fakenham Local History Society. The main panel facing the street is obvious enough, a reminder of the town's printing history, but the penny-farthing, the covered waggon, the ship? Even the plough, which turns up on so many signs, has a deeper meaning here; it represents the farm workers' leader, Sir George Edwards, who became a local M.P.

The others symbolise local people too. The waggon is for the Revd Henry Buckenham, Methodist missionary in Africa, the penny-farthing is for John Garrood, engineer and bicycle-maker, and the ship is for Sir Robert Seppings, master shipwright and Surveyor of the Navy. Finally the Quaker on the large reverse panel is Edmund Peckover, one of whose descendants opened Fakenham's first bank, and the coat of arms is of the Duchy of Lancaster, former holder of the Manor. Any questions?

This glass fibre replica of Harry Carter's original wooden sign was painted by the local schoolchildren and erected in time for the Millennium.

FELBRIGG

Here is a considerable rarity, a sign erected at the end of 1999 which does not commemorate the Millennium; the villagers just wanted a village sign. It is also rather unusual in costing only £100 - including the unveiling party!

An amateur wood-carver in Felbrigg, Ivan Pardon, had always wanted to make one, and he gave his services, plus the wood. The wooden post came form an oak tree given by the National Trust, owners of Felbrigg Hall, which is the centrepiece of the sign. It was built for the Windham family in the 1620s and left to the Trust by the writer R.W.Ketton-Cremer in 1969. The oak leaves on the sign are not only the Trust's emblem but also represent Felbrigg's woods, and the ram's head is doubly symbolic - it represents Weaver's Way which passes through the village, and livestock breeding which is important locally.

Between them is a copy of the brass in the parish church to Sir Symon de Felbrigg, the earliest portrait of a local resident. He was royal standard-bearer to King Richard II - but still found time to build the church.

FELTWELL

Harry Carter's wooden sign of 1969 was replaced by a metal one a couple of years ago, but its main features are much the same, except for the central figure of Alveva, the Saxon lady who owned part of the original town of Feltwell. Harry depicted her as a buxom and rather sexy young lady, but she has matured considerably in thirty years and now has rather fewer curves and a less inviting expression. Her dogs, however, look quite resigned to it.

So does the ancient oak behind her, said to have been 1300 years old when it was felled in 1964. In the background is St Nicholas's church before its tower collapsed in 1898, and the sheep recall the large flocks that used to be kept on the local estates, but the shepherd's crook carved on the post represents a shepherd called Edward Atmere who founded a local charity. The coats of arms, one of which is rather endearingly decorated with three cats' heads and three paw-marks, belong to the families who founded the other charities, the Moundefords and the Cloughs. The Moundeford almshouses still bear witness to their generosity, just behind the sign.

GARVESTONE

For as long as anyone can remember there has been a debate about the 'e' in Garvestone, so a village survey was carried out before the sign was made, and an overwhelming majority said the 'e' should be included. So that is how it is spelt, and maybe the debate is now over. On the other hand, maybe not.

There has also been some doubt about the name's origin. The W.I.'s Norfolk Village Book says it comes from *Ger* or *Gar*, the original spelling of the River Yare which flows through the village. However, some experts say the original Gerolfstuna meant Geirulft's or Gaerwulf's enclosure, which could be Old English, or Old Norse, or a bit of both. Either way, the sign has a longboat which is said to be Saxon - but then again it could be Danish...

The other illustrations are uncontroversial: the parish church, the local shop, and Garvestone's traditional red telephone box - perhaps to honour the fact the telephone directory always spells Garvestone with an 'e'.

HAPPISBURGH

Happisburgh's two best-known features, to mariners as well as landlubbers, are its church and its lighthouse, and both have a place on the sign. Their different forms of guiding light have not always been effective, judging by the graves in the churchyard of hundreds of sailors who have fallen foul of the notorious Haisbro Sands over the centuries, but they do make striking landmarks.

The sign's centrepiece has a less obvious significance; it depicts a baptism service, a familiar scene in every parish church. But it is the officiating parson whom it particularly commemorates, the eighteenth century Revd Thomas Lloyd, who was so worried about the lack of local interest in baptisms that he offered to provide entertainment and hospitality after the service to any couples who brought babies for baptism on Whit Sunday, 1793. The response was overwhelming. For the first and last time at Happisburgh, there were 120 baptisms in one day. No wonder the other two figures on the sign, the eleventh-century overlord Edric the Dane, and the later Lady of the Manor, Maud Bigod, have turned away in disbelief.

HOLT

HEMPNALL

The preacher on the sign brandishing a Bible in front of a modest audience was a well-known figure throughout England in the 1700s, and it was therefore quite an occasion for Hempnall when John Wesley walked ten miles from Norwich to conduct a service on the village green. However, the chap at the back with the horn was not giving him a welcoming fanfare. He and other hecklers were there to interrupt the service. But Wesley was used to this sort of thing, and a plaque records the relevant entry in his diary: 'The ringleader of the mob came with his horn, as usual, before I began, but one quickly catched and threw away his horn, and in a few minutes he was deserted by all his companions, who were seriously attentive to the great truth: "By Grace ye are saved through faith".'

It so happened that when a village sign was being discussed, the local historian was a descendant of Wesley's sister Susannah. Hence his reappearance in Hempnall, two centuries later.

Holt originally had one of Harry Carter's elaborate double-sided signs from the 1970s, but the Norfolk weather was too much for it. It featured two very contrasting local characters, Sir Thomas Gresham, founder of Gresham's School, and on the other side Lady Alice Perrers, a maid of honour to Queen Philippa who became Edward III's mistress. Now she and Sir Thomas have retired together, albeit still back to back, to sheltered accommodation at his School, and they have been replaced by a new sign in the shape of a tree, a reminder that the Old English *holt* meant a thicket or a wood.

It has however retained one distinctive feature of its predecessor. On the tree is perched an owl like the one that, according to local tradition, was found wandering into the town and for its own safety was put in the pound, where stray animals were kept. In due course it flew off, but it is remembered in the names of the town football team, one of the WIs, and other establishments in Holt. Unfortunately the owl 'flew off' again recently, following damage by vandals, but it is being replaced.

KETTLESTONE

A rare gyrfalcon, so rare in medieval times that only royalty could own them, is the central feature of the sign, recalling that a thirteenth-century Lord of the Manor, Sir Thomas de Hauville, was Keeper of the King's Falcons. It has been suggested that Sir Thomas climbed the church tower (in the background on the sign) to observe the birds, but I have had to climb several church towers in the course of duty, and I suspect he had the good sense to send up his falconer instead...

The de Hauville shield is on the sign, together with that of the Montagues, another prominent local family; Sir Thomas's, of course, is the one with the falcon. But rather more unusual than the sign itself is the story behind it.

At the age of sixty Mrs Marjorie Santer (who lives, inevitably, in Claus Cottage) rode her tiny moped, still bearing L-plates, from Kettlestone to Caernarvon, following an 800-mile route along minor roads, to raise money for the sign. To cap it, in a village competition with entrants unidentified, her design was selected to go on the sign. In her book *Ride a Red Moped* she ends: 'I pass the sign often and the falcon looks down at me fiercely - but I like to fancy we have a special relationship!'

KIMBERLEY

The imposing coat of arms was originally on the gateway to Kimberley Park, once the ancestral home of the Wodehouse family. In 1960 it was donated to the village by the then Baron Wodehouse, Earl of Kimberley, thus providing a ready-made village sign.

The arms were granted to Sir John Wodehouse by Henry V in recognition of his valour at Agincourt. To me its most fascinating feature is not the shield but the two figures supporting it, muscular gentlemen with very large clubs and very small knickers. They were 'wild men of the woods' who appear on a number of church fonts in Norfolk, notably Happisburgh, and as far afield as Staple in Kent. Even there they were known as 'wodehouses'.

It is more usual to find lions, unicorns, horses, even dogs acting as heraldic guardians. Why, one wonders, did Sir John select such bizarre characters, often associated with pagan religious rites? I am sure that one of his twentieth-century kinsmen, the late P.G.Wodehouse, could have devised a wonderfully entertaining explanation to link these half-naked clubmen with a different kind of clubman in Norfolk's county families.

LITCHAM

This very practical combination of village sign and village noticeboard features Matthew Halcott, the master tanner who was so delighted when Charles II was restored to the throne that he paid for the little bell-cote on the church to be replaced by a full-scale church tower. A lengthy poem in the Archdeacon's Register at the time pays tribute to his generosity. It ends:

'Yea, as long as Litcham stand, when he is rotten,
This good work of his shall not be forgotten'.

Archdeacons' Registers in those days, it seems, were a little more entertaining than they are today.

The benefactor was one of a series of Matthew Halcotts, fathers and sons, who lived in Litcham for 150 years. The tannery was at Priory Farm, formerly a hermit's chapel where pilgrims were offered rest and refreshment at the river crossing on their way to Walsingham. It still stands by the bridge but is now a private residence.

Sir Thomas Felton, a Lord of the Manor who fought gallantly at the Battle of Crécy, has his coat of arms below the noticeboard, but the top billing goes to Matthew Halcott, in honour of one the few church towers to be built at the cost of a tanner.

LONG STRATTON

To frustrated motorists crawling through Long Stratton on the congested A140 trunk road to Norwich, the stationary wheel on the village sign may be a painful reminder of how slowly their own wheels are turning, but it actually dates back long before the days of the car. It is a replica of the medieval sexton's wheel in St Mary's Church, one of only two in the country that still survive. The other is at Yaxley in Suffolk.

Actually it is two wheels fitted together which can revolve either way. It was used rather like one of those 'Wheels of Chance' on a fairground, but for the much loftier purpose of deciding which day to observe a penance knows as the Madonna's Fast. Each section represented a day sacred to the Madonna, and a piece of string was attached to a hole in each one. The sexton spun the wheel and the prospective penitent grabbed one of the strings as they all flew round. The section it was attached to gave the day of the fast.

The original iron wheel in the church is now as motionless as the teak one on the sign. Locals could argue that unless their campaign for a bypass soon succeeds, a lot more wheels in Long Stratton will come to a standstill too.

LUDHAM

King Canute, the central figure on the sign, has had a mixed press over the centuries. The tabloids have mocked him over his much-publicised encounter with the incoming tide, and more serious critics have accused him of the standard Danish rape and pillage. The pro-Canute lobby, however, regard him as a wise and god-fearing monarch - and that includes the monks of nearby St Benet's Abbey, in his day a Benedictine monastery.

The enthroned king is handing one of the monks a charter which gave them the Manor of Ludham, one of their many local estates. But there are mixed views about his relationship with the Abbey. Some say he rebuilt it after it was destroyed by his forebears in an earlier Danish invasion, but it has also been suggested that he burned it down himself, then had a change of heart and rebuilt it on a more lavish scale.

Either way, the monks look very happy about it. On the other side of the king, St Catherine, patron saint of Ludham church, is leaning on the wheel which is the symbol of her eventual martyrdom. Understandably she looks as if she has other things to worry about.

LYNG

The date above the sign is 1980, but the sign itself was only made and installed inside the original framework last year. It is much more detailed than the old one, which simply depicted in black metalwork the bridge across the river by the old mill. This was where, according to tradition, the 18th century diarist Parson Woodforde bought some faulty writing paper that just absorbed the ink. But it proved useful nonetheless. Years ahead of paper towels and tissues, Lyng Mill had produced the first blotting paper!

The bridge and mill appear again on the new sign, but it also has the former nunnery known as St Edmund's Chapel, complete with nuns, the parish church of St Margaret's, a forge, a haycart, and bunches of lyng, the Oldf Norse name for heather, from which some say the village got its name.

Also featured is Humphrey Repton, the 18thcentury landscape gardener, who is said to have had a hand in designing the gardens at the Old Rectory. Mr Bob Holland, the former parish clerk who voluntarily designed and painted the sign, used a little artistic licence and put him in Tudor costume. He also took the trouble to paint a complete list of Lyng Rectors on the back of the sign, going back to the thirteenth century.

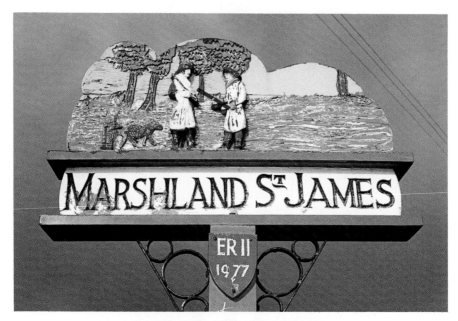

MARSHLAND ST JAMES

Marshland St James may seem a little off the beaten track, but in the days of West Norfolk's famous giant-killer Tom Hickathrift it was on his route to Wisbech, delivering barrels of beer from King's Lynn - and according to the sign this was where he found his way blocked by the giant, wielding a hefty club. But even at the age of ten, so it is said, Tom had been able to pick up an entire wagon-load of straw in one go. As a young man, when told he could take as much firewood as he could carry, in payment for a day's work, he uprooted a fair-sized tree and took it home over his shoulder. So a giant – even a giant with a hefty club – was no problem. According to legend Tom took a wheel off his cart to act as a shield and used the axle as a stave to vanquish the giant. Then he filled his cart with gold and silver from the giant's cave and lived happily ever after.

The back of the sign depicts another large gentleman called Nonsuch in presumably an earlier confrontation with the giant. But Nonsuch did not leave behind as many reminders of his existence as Tom, who is said to have modelled for the muscular effigy on the wall of Walpole St Peter church. There are two or three large stones in the area known as Hickathrift's Candlesticks, and an outsize coffin-lid in Tilney All Saints church is reputed to have marked his grave. Should we regard Nonsuch, I wonder, as No-such?

MATTISHALL

The glass-fibre drum-shaped sign caused quite a local controversy when it was erected in a specially-created alcove in the churchyard wall. Traditionalists said it was vulgar to use 'plastic', and altering the wall was 'desecration', but happily things have quietened down since then. When I first saw it I confess I was tempted to suggest that the top of the sign ought to revolve, but that really would stir things up again....

Each panel has a different spelling of the village's name since it evolved from the Domesday Book's Mateshala . The front panel depicts Matthew Parker, the Norwich-born Archbishop of Canterbury, whose close watch on his clergy originated the term 'Nosey Parker'. He married a Mattishall woman, Margaret Harlestone, who left a bequest for the Parker Sermon, which is still preached at Rogationtide.

On another panel is one of the little tumbrels made in the village for over a century by the Dobbs family, and a third shows a mule-train led by a local wool dealer or 'brogger' - the term was not entirely polite. On the last panel is a Roman pot containing 1100 silver coins uncovered on a building site in 1968.

MELTON CONSTABLE

The village used to be the mid-Norfolk centre for the Midland & Great Northern Joint Railway, brought here by Lord Hastings of Melton Constable Hall. With its construction and repair sheds and its terraced rows of railway cottages, it was known as the Crewe of Norfolk, and the M & G N steam engine on the sign is a reminder of those busy days. Then rural railways declined, Dr Beeching finished them off, and the M & G N's affectionate nickname, 'Muddle & Go Nowhere', became a sad reality.

The tower on the other side of the sign dates back much earlier. Variously known as the Belle Vue Tower, the Hastings Tower, or just 'That Tower', it was built in 1721 as a smock windmill, the highest-sited mill in Norfolk. Sixty years later Sir Edward Astley, a forebear of Lord Hastings, decided to rebuild and heighten the upper part as a six-storey lookout tower. It is not clear why he wanted one – a mill seems a lot more useful twenty miles from the sea – but whatever the Astleys wanted to have on their land, be it railways or lookout towers, nobody in Melton Constable was likely to argue. It was restored twenty years ago as an unusual private residence.

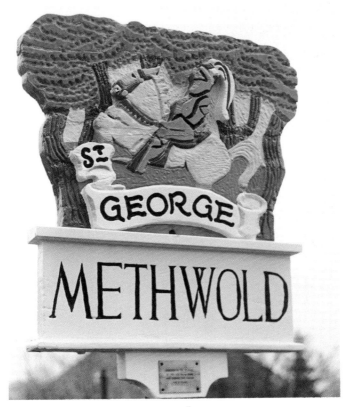

METHWOLD

Methwold has two or three events in its history which might have qualified for the village sign – not least the Methwold Fruit Farm Colony, founded in 1889 by a London businessman who reckoned anyone could live off two or three acres of land, by eating what produce they needed and selling the rest. He managed it himself, but many 'colonists' did not, and the project died. Only its name, Brookfield, survives.

Instead of this ill-fated venture the sign remembers a much-loved figure of more recent years. It was erected in 1970 ' to the memory of the late Nurse Hunt, who served this parish for 31 years'. She died on St George's Day, hence his figure on the sign.

St George is also patron saint of the parish church, where there is another odd little tale from Methwold's past. The fourteenth century brass of Sir Adam de Clifton was stolen in 1680 and sold to a tinker. Surprisingly it was recovered – but in 130 pieces. The jigsaw was painstakingly reassembled, but inevitably there were gaps that had to be painted in. It would be nice to think that, up there on the sign, St George is gallantly riding off to find the missing pieces...

MIDDLETON

So much village history is packed on to the two sides of the sign it is difficult to know where to start. There are four main scenes, representing the four hamlets that make up the parish: Middleton, Tower End, Blackborough End and Fair Green, each with its own tale to tell. Any gaps are filled in on the four shields underneath the main cameos.

Middleton itself is represented by the hill fort that used to stand on the ancient motte known as Middleton Mount, with an imposing warrior in the foreground defending it. Beside him in the next segment is the seventh Lord Scales, looking a little more welcoming in front of Middleton Towers, the impressive manor house he built at Tower End. On the other side of the sign is a nun, her hands together in prayer, in front of the former nunnery at Blackborough End. Next to her is a rather different character, a customer clutching a tankard outside the Gate Inn.

The shields feature a Bronze Age jewel, Roman coins, the Scales arms, a silver fox from the fox farm and a horse from the Fair Green horse fair. And the tree in the middle? I think it's just a tree...

NARBOROUGH

This ingenious sign is in the shape of the mill wheel that survived from Narborough's old bone mill, where bones were crushed for fertiliser. The spokes divide it into six segments, each one containing a reminder of a different aspect of the village over the years.

One of them, predictably, is Narborough Hall, once the home of the Spelman family, headed by the judge who prepared the indictment against Anne Boleyn and was given the Manor of Narborough by Henry VIII as a reward. Other segments have the parish church, where many of the Spelmans are buried, the cornmill and the maltings.

From more recent times there is a train crossing a bridge - the line closed in 1968 - and a first World War plane flying over a hangar. Narborough Aerodrome has long since been overtaken by the vast RAF station at nearby Marham, but in its day it was one of the largest and most important in the county. It covered more than 900 acres, a quarter of the whole parish. Today all that is left of its hundred-odd buildings is one lonely shed.

NORDELPH

Nordelph has a Dutch-sounding name, some Dutch-looking buildings, and a Dutch-looking scene on one side of its village sign, depicting speed skaters on what could be a frozen Dutch waterway, but is actually Well Creek. This area was in fact much populated in the seventeenth century by the Dutch workers who came over with Cornelius Vermuyden to drain the Fens.

The other side of the sign is more typically Norfolk, a lone ploughman behind his horse-drawn plough, but even this is unusual. A passing villager pointed out to me that the plough is 'right-hand drive'; the plough's blade is actually to the left of the horse and the ploughman. 'I hent never seen a plough like that in these parts,' he told me, and I met others in Nordelph who were equally sceptical.

However the sign was made by the normally very accurate Harry Carter, whose work is all over the county. This was one of his last ones - he retired the following year - and I would like to think that the mistake, if it was one, was intentional, just to see if people like me would spot it...

OLD CATTON

Old Catton's name has only a tenuous link with cats. According to the experts it comes from *Catestuna*, or Catta's settlement, and the theory is that this was the founder's nickname, as *catt* is Old English for a wildcat, and he may have shown the same characteristics. Nevertheless the combination of a cat and a tun, or barrel, was too obvious a pun to miss, and there they are on the pillar, not just painted or carved on a background but an actual barrel surmounted by an actual wooden cat. They replaced a previous cat and barrel, which were erected to mark King George V's silver jubilee in 1935.

During the war, when signposts were taken down to confuse any invaders, Old Catton's sign was taken down too, and apparently had a number of adventures before finally disappearing in the 1950s.

The present one was donated by a generous Danish visitor, who is reported to have said that a Danish cat would feel at home in a former Danish settlement. As I understand it, the cat in *catestuna* was actually English, but it was a kind thought anyway.

OUTWELL

The post on which Outwell's two-sided sign normally stands was alarmingly bare when I was there last October, and I feared it might have been snatched by sign-rustlers, but happily it was only in neighbouring Upwell, being spruced up for the Millennium.

One side depicts the former Beaupré Hall with its turreted gatehouse, the Elizabethan home of the Beaupré family. The other shows a very contrasting style of architecture, the aqueduct which carries Well Creek over the Middle Level Drain, part of the artificial waterway system which drains the Fens.

'Well' in this sense is a confusing word. In Old English it meant 'stream', so Upwell means 'further upstream', and Outwell probably came later, 'outside Upwell'. Well Creek must literally mean 'stream stream'; it is certainly twice the size of most streams, large enough to take commercial barges like the one on the sign. These days it is used more by holiday craft. When it froze over in very hard winters it had another recreational use, for speed skating. But to see that on a village sign you have to go further 'downwell' to Nordelph.

OVERSTRAND

This is a replacement for another Harry Carter sign from the 1970s, which succumbed a few years ago to the wear and tear of wind, weather and salt water, a destructive combination along this stretch of coast. The design of the new one is based on ideas put forward by local schoolchildren, and it paints a rather more mellow picture of the village than its predecessor.

The old sign mainly concentrated on the more dramatic aspects of Overstrand's history. One side featured a shipwreck with a lone survivor struggling up the cliff. The other had a Saxon and a Viking glaring at each other belligerently, a ruined church about to fall into the sea, and Black Shuck, a legendary hound said to haunt the area – 'an awful creature, as black as ebony, whose fiendish howls have been heard above the shrieks of the wildest gales' – or as one local described it to the writer R.H.Mottram: 'A gre't ole dawg wi' no head but tew blazing eyes.'

The new sign, in contrast, shows the present church and a pleasant view of the runway down to the beach. But it also includes some smaller features from the previous one – a crab representing the local crab-fishing industry, a poppy for 'Poppyland', and the emblem of the Women's Institute, which was the original donor.

PORINGLAND

When the Norwich artist John Crome decided it would be rather nice to paint an oak tree he had several well-known ones in Norfolk to choose from, ranging from the assortment of 'Kett's Oaks' scattered around Norfolk under which the rebel leader rallied his followers, to the 'Bale Oak', reputed to be the oldest in the county and large enough to accommodate a cobbler's shop in its hollow trunk. Instead, however, he chose an oak tree at Poringland, and in doing so he made it more famous than any of the others. The Poringland Oak is now in the National Gallery, and since it is the village's main claim to glory it was chosen to feature on the sign, complete with Mr Crome working at his easel.

As for the original Poringland Oak, there is one in Carr's Lane, just outside the village, which has been referred to in the past as 'Old Crome's Oak', but there is no evidence that this was the one. Certainly there seems very little similarity. The sign, however, is a handsome substitute.

POTTER HEIGHAM

The village has two signs, very colourful and attractive, but the one by the famous bridge is perhaps more for the tourists as they flock on to the bridge to watch yet another novice boatman crash into it. This sign predictably shows sailing boats and a windmill on one side, and on the other the Roman potters who gave the village its name.

The sign in the old village is rather more intriguing. Again it has on one side a sailing boat and a windmill, this time with some corn-stacks and a ploughman, but on the reverse is a drummer in an army uniform of Wellington's day - wearing skates.

According to local legend a regiment was stationed on the far side of Hickling Broad, and one of the soldiers formed an attachment with a Potter Heigham girl. When the Broad froze over he decided to take a short cut across it at night to meet her. Alas, one night a thaw set in, the ice gave way, and he was drowned. It is said that on some winter's nights a ghostly drummer can be seen on Hickling Broad, a grim warning of the dangers of skating on thin ice. Perhaps the tourists ought to see this sign too.

PULHAM ST MARY

The two identical airships on the sign, one on each side, were built in vast hangars at Pulham after the First World War. In 1919 the R34 flew successfully to America and back; it is depicted with a cheering crowd seeing it off. That was the good news. The bad news came seven years later, when its sister ship the R33 was being prepared for its final trials, tethered to its mast, with twenty people on board.

The cloud painted above it on the sign may be a hint of what was to come. The wind suddenly strengthened and flung it against the mooring mast, snapping the connecting arm and crushing the airship's nose section. It was blown out to sea and nearly reached Holland before the crew regained control and managed to fly it back home. No one was hurt, but it was a foretaste of a far worse disaster.

In 1930 the R101 crashed in France on its maiden flight from Cardington in Bedfordshire, with the loss of nearly fifty lives. The age of the airship was ending - but at Pulham St Mary it is not forgotten. The sign was erected in 1977 and repainted just a few years ago.

QUIDENHAM

The figure on the sign is unmistakeable, the intrepid Boadicea (or for the pedantic, Boudicca), Queen of the Iceni, who was maltreated by the Romans and wreaked a spectacular revenge. Spoilsport historians have cast doubt on the scythes on her chariot-wheels, but with or without their benefit she slaughtered the Roman inhabitants of Colchester, St Albans and London. Here she stands in her war chariot, her spear at the ready, driving a pair of spirited horses - every inch the Warrior Queen.

Her connection with Quidenham, one has to say, is a little tenuous. She is believed to have had a palace at neighbouring Kenninghall, and legend has it that she lies buried beneath a lofty pine-covered mound by the River Whittle, not far from Quidenham church. But the mound has also been described as a round barrow, which could put it much earlier than Boadicea and the Romans, and on some maps it is marked as 'Viking's Mound', which would put it much later. Some ley-hunters also claim that it lies on a prehistoric ley-line, along which energy currents still flow.

However, as nobody can prove any of these theories, let's give Boadicea - and the Quidenham sign - the benefit of the doubt.

REEPHAM

This is one of those rare and entirely delightful signs which look as if they must have some deep significance originating in the mists of local history, and in fact are just attractive generalised impressions of nothing in particular.

The old sign, which had to be replaced some years ago, depicted the two churches which still stand in the churchyard – a third was burnt down in the sixteenth century. The Reepham Society held a competition for a new design and it was won by the High School, which produced this rural scene. The three churches in the background are logical enough, but I am assured that the other groups of threes dotted about the landscape – three monks, three farm workers, three cows, three sheep – are just there for artistic decoration. Even the three ladies in the foreground, who might have represented the (quite unfounded) legend of the three sisters who built the churches, have no intentional connection.

It all adds up to an entertaining riddle for the casual visitor – and a distinct hazard for unwary compilers of books about Norfolk signs.

SEA PALLING

Sea Palling's eight-oared lifeboat played its part in saving hundreds of lives before engine power took over, and it is portrayed dramatically on the sign, climbing a mountainous wave. It was funded locally until the RNLI took it over in 1858. The station was closed in the 1930s, but in recent times an inflatable craft has been manned by the Palling Volunteer Rescue Service, maintaining the local tradition of saving lives at sea. No one could help, though, when the sea struck the village itself during the 1953 floods, and seven people died.

Below the lifeboat the fishes and the sheaf of corn represent fishing and farming, and the key is often associated with St Peter. The parish church is actually dedicated to St Margaret, but it does have a very ancient key.

Incidentally the mountainous wave on the sign also provides the 'Sea' in Sea Palling; the wording on the sign is limited to Palling. I prefer the longer version, not least because if I lived in the village I would not want it mocked as 'just a Palling....'

49

SEDGEFORD

Sedgeford has the unusual luxury for a small village of two village signs. The Women's Institute not only paid for them both but also provided the designs - one was by their secretary, the other by their president.

On one there are a lamb and a sheaf of corn, representing local agriculture, the other features a curious-looking house with an even more curious history. 'The Magazine' is reputed to have been an arms store during the Civil War, but opinions seem to differ on which side used it. The popular theory is that it belonged to the Royalist Lord of the Manor of Hunstanton, Hamon Lestrange, but when it was sold a few years ago it was called 'a former Cromwellian arms store'.

Its design, however, is very odd for an arms store, with its mullioned windows and tall, thin chimneys, and a third theory has been put forward. Could it have been just a Victorian 'folly'?

Whatever it was, it is now a Grade II listed building, its recent asking price was nearly £130,000, and it has achieved immortality on a village sign.

SHOULDHAM

The village was once a thriving market town with two annual fairs, and as a reminder the sign has three sheep, a couple of cows and a horse, all being driven to market by a versatile drover. They have been halted, apparently by a large monk, far taller even than the horse - for a final blessing, perhaps, or just a donation?

He and the ruined archway behind him symbolise Shouldham's thirteenth-century Gilbertine double monastery, the only one of its kind in Norfolk. This was the only medieval religious order founded in England, named after a Lincolnshire priest who started it off, Gilbert of Sempringham. Unusually for such an Order, its monks observed the rule of the Augustinians while the nuns observed that of the Benedictines. The combination must have worked: the Gilbertines established twenty-five priories before they were dissolved at the Reformation, along with all the others. At Shouldham today, not even a ruined archway survives.

The well depicted beneath the sign was fed by water containing a mineral which formed a silvery scum. Inevitably it was known as the 'Silver Well', but alas, the scum was probably just scum.

SNETTISHAM

The centrepiece of the sign looks rather like a mis-shapen horseshoe, but not many horseshoes are made of gold, like the original of this. It dates back to the Anglo-Saxon settlement which gave Snettisham its name, 'Snet's homestead'. Snet established it very close to the site of an earlier Roman outpost, and over the years many relics have been unearthed from both periods, from Roman coins to Saxon combs. The sign recalls perhaps the most spectacular discovery, a golden Celtic torque, and at the time this ancient necklet was indeed the torque of the county. It was given a place of honour in Norwich Castle Museum, and subsequently the prime position on the village sign.

Below are the more familiar symbols of a seaside village, a couple of sea-horses and a rather less expensive necklet made of cockle shells. The other main figures on the sign were also a familiar sight around the Norfolk coast a couple of centuries ago. On either side of their square-rigged boat are two smugglers, one laden with contraband, the other armed with a pistol and apparently celebrating with a passable imitation of a hornpipe.

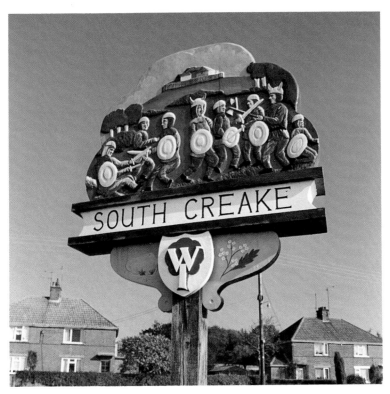

SOUTH CREAKE

The design on one side of the sign applies to most Norfolk villages. It shows the parish church with a ploughman in the foreground, both playing vital roles in village life. The other side is more unusual, a battle between early Britons and Danes in front of a hill fort just outside the village. Legend has it that the slaughter was so great that blood flowed down the hill, and it is still known as Bloodgate.

The tankard on the sign recalls, not the victory celebration after the battle, but just the local brewery - not quite as intriguing as the packet of 'Farmer's Glory' wheat flakes, representing one of the more innovative industries which used to flourish in South Creake. (In 1921, for instance, the brewery was converted into a razor-blade factory, which was still in production during the last war.) Meanwhile the Alley brothers made Bluestone Farm the first fully mechanised farm in the country, then produced one of England's earliest breakfast cereals to fight back against Dr Kellogg and his colleagues from across the Atlantic, just as those much earlier Britons battled against another invader. That 'Farmer's Glory' packet deserves its posthumous glory alongside them on the sign.

53

SOUTH WALSHAM

The longboat and warrior in the foreground recall the Danish invasions that Norfolk frequently endured, a fairly common theme on signs where villages had navigable rivers nearby. Rather less common are the two church towers at the back, because, like the churches at Reepham they share the same churchyard.

The story goes that the Lord of the Manor left his estate equally between two daughters, and each decided to build her own church on the same site. But one sister was much nastier than the other and consequently her church was 'doomed'. Certainly St Lawrence's was gutted by fire in 1827, and although it was partly restored a combination of lightning and sonic boom in 1971 wrecked the tower. These days the neighbouring St Mary's is the parish church and St Lawrence's has been restored as an arts centre.

The Tale of Two Sisters is appealing, but I am afraid it is more likely that St Lawrence's was built first, probably on a pagan sacred site, and when the parish was divided the second church used the same sacred ground. As for St Lawrence being doomed, it all depends how you interpret 'Acts of God'...

STIBBARD

Fred the Ploughman is unique in Norfolk and probably in the country. He was created from junked farm implements with great ingenuity and a skilfully-handled soldering-iron by a well-known local sculptress, Ros Newman, and it is an interesting exercise to try to identify all the bits and pieces that have gone into his skeletal figure. I managed to spot two pitchforks, four horseshoes, a tail-docker, a pair of pincers, some chain-link, a couple of branding-irons and a sugar-beet hook. His hollow head is protected by a wartime tin hat, and his plough is a real one. He stands on a handsome pedestal opposite the site of the village pound.

Fred is a great contrast to the more familiar carved signs of Harry Carter and others. He has attracted great attention over the years, and there are some very solemn interpretations of what he symbolises - the spirit of Norfolk agriculture, perhaps, epitomising the constant struggle to till the land in all weathers to provide our daily bread. I am sure that is so. But to me he is just Fred the Ploughman, another great old Norfolk character.

STIFFKEY

The sign says both 'Stiffkey' and 'Stewkey', but Stewkey only refers to the famous cockles which the women are shown gathering on the beach. As well as the Stewkey Blues the sign features samphire or sea asparagus, another succulent local product. There is a silver chalice and the emblems of St John's and St Mary's churches, which shared the churchyard until St Mary's collapsed a century ago, and the boar is a punning reminder of the Bacon family who used to live at the Old Hall.

But what of the local Rector who became even better known in more recent years than even those cockles? The Revd Harold Davidson, 'The Prostitute's Padre', spent much of his time in London rescuing fallen women, and in due course was accused of immoral practices and defrocked, although he always protested his innocence. He was still doing so from inside a lion's cage at Skegness when the cage's other occupant attacked and killed him.

It is perhaps understandable that he does not appear on the sign. But there could be a discreet way of remembering him in view of his dramatic end. After all, lots of village signs feature a rampant lion...

SWAFFHAM

This was Harry Carter's first sign, which he presented to the town where he was art and woodwork master at Hamond's Grammar School. He went on to make scores more, for towns and villages all over Norfolk and beyond.

His Swaffham sign depicts 'Ye Pedlar of Swaffham who did by a dream find a great treasure'. According to legend a pedlar called John Chapman dreamed that he should go to London Bridge where he would learn how to acquire a fortune. He duly went, and there he met a stranger who said that he too had had a dream that if he went to somewhere called Swaffham and dug in a certain garden - he described Chapman's garden in detail - he would find a crock of gold. The stranger, being a sophisticated Londoner, said he did not believe in dreams and anyway he had never heard of Swaffham. Sensible fellow, said Chapman, then headed back home, dug his garden and found not just one crock of gold, but two.

Some say this was only a parable to illustrate 'There's no place like home'. But there really was a John Chapman (whose name meant 'pedlar'), he certainly acquired a fortune, and he became a great benefactor to the church and town. So who knows?

THETFORD

They must be very fair-minded folk in Thetford. Of all the distinguished characters who have been associated with the town over the centuries, from King Edmund the Martyr to the Maharajah Duleep Singh, they selected for their town sign two men who were undoubtedly the most unpopular figures of their time. One is Swein Forkbeard, the Danish invader who sacked the town during one of the many Viking invasions, and the other is the radical writer Thomas Paine, who supported the American colonists against the English and attacked the Royal Family and hereditary rule – to such a degree that even the normally benevolent Arthur Mee in his book on Norfolk referred to him as 'the completest specimen of that rare creature, a renegade Englishman'.

Paine has become accepted now, and in fact Thetford also has a statue to him – though admittedly presented by an American. But it seems ironic that old Forkbeard should feature under the town arms showing Castle Hill, which was used successively by early Britons, Romans, Saxons and Normans to defend Thetford against marauders.

THOMPSON

The Roman soldier, the pilgrim and the goosegirl have only one thing in common – except perhaps sore feet. They all walked the Peddars Way, the ancient track linking the Icknield Way at Thetford with the North Norfolk coast. It dates back to prehistoric times, so an Ancient Briton would have qualified for the sign too. These days the Peddars Way sees rather fewer travellers; it runs along the boundary between Thompson and the Stanford Training Area, occupied by the army since 1942.

Compared with the three colourful hikers, the shield underneath them may seem rather dull, but this too has a tale to tell. It bears the coat of arms of the Shardelows, former Lords of the Manor, and behind it is the seal of the college that was founded at Thompson by Sir Thomas and John de Shardelow, two pious brothers, in 1349. It incorporated the newly-built church close by, which still has evidence of its former collegiate status. There was a Master and five other brethren, and the college flourished for nearly two hundred years until it was dissolved during the Reformation. Its remains form part of what is now College Farm.

THORNHAM

Reminders of the past range from the old post-mill that blew down in 1928 to the ship's bell from the village's namesake, the minesweeper HMS *Thornham*, which now hangs in the church. But the picture of what looks like a large village smithy needs rather more explanation.

This was Thornham Ironworks, founded by the Lady of the Manor in 1887 to provide an evening activity for the men of the village. It grew from a part-time hobby into an international business employing over thirty workers, making anything from pub signs to church lecterns; there are local examples at the King's Head and All Saints' Church. But their most successful product was garden gates, and after making a set for Sandringham their fame spread much further. They exhibited at the 1900 Paris Exhibition and at the Brussels Exhibition a year later, where they won a gold medal.

The founder, Mrs Ames Lyde, remained the driving force, but she died in 1914, the men went off to war, and a few years later the most remarkable 'village smithy' in Norfolk despatched its final set of gates – and closed its own.

THURSFORD

Think of almost any aspect of village life and you will find it represented here. The church? There is the flag of its patron saint, St Andrew. The squire? It has the arms of the Chad family. Agriculture? A ploughman on one side, a horse and cart on the other. Plus a barrel for the pubs, a blackboard and easel for the school, an anvil for the blacksmith, an oak for the nearby woods, and a railway engine for the Midland & Great Northern Line. But the traction engine has a more unusual tale to tell.

It represents, not just a local threshing business, but the Thursford Collection, founded by Mr George Cushing with the traction engines he loved, and now a remarkable assemblage of giant mechanical organs and roundabouts as well as engines, with a Mighty Wurlitzer Organ as the centrepiece. Every year Mr Cushing's son stages a Christmas spectacular involving the exhibits, with a cast ranging from a flight of doves to human snowmen – and it's always a sell-out.

It was the Cushings, incidentally, who donated the village sign – but they refrained from including any snowmen...

WACTON

Most of the illustrations on the sign are straightforward enough. Dominating it is the seventeenth-century postmill, and below that is a ploughing scene and the parish church. But who is the furtive fellow in the barrel? A drunken pirate perhaps?

Not exactly. This is John Aylmer, the Norfolk-born tutor to the ill-fated Lady Jane Grey who must have had quite a crush on him. 'I think myself in hell,' she wrote, 'till the time comes that I must go to Mr Aylmer, who teaches me so gently, so pleasantly, and with such fair allurements to learning that I think all the time nothing while I am with him...'

Under the Catholic Queen Mary the charismatic Mr Aylmer had to flee the country, reputedly hidden in a barrel - hence the sign - but he returned after her death and became Bishop of London. According to the sign he was born at Wacton. Unfortunately the reference books are pretty well unanimous that he was born at Tilney St Lawrence - and he features on that sign too!

Luckily the villages are more than forty miles apart, and if there has been any dispute over their signs - well, I have found no sign of it.

WALPOLE CROSS KEYS

The story of King John losing his treasure in the Wash has been adapted to include various Norfolk villages over the centuries. Some say, for instance, that the treasure was actually buried at Walpole St Andrew and never reached the Wash at all. Walpole Cross Keys, on the other hand, reckons he still had it with him when he passed through the village, and when the Women's Institute organised a village sign to go in the little war memorial garden opposite the Woolpack Inn, that is the theme they chose.

So there is the King riding by, accompanied only by a rather morose donkey with a heavy load on his back. Could it be, I wonder, that it was the rest of his entourage, not the treasure, that got lost in the Wash? Perhaps the sign can start a new version of the legend.

In the bottom corners are a daffodil and a strawberry, symbolising the main crops in the area. The maple leaf and the rose in the top corners may therefore be puzzling, particularly the leaf, since maple trees are not common in West Norfolk, but these are in fact the emblems of England and Canada, where the W.I. movement began.

WATTON

Like several other Norfolk places ending in 'ton', Watton has a sign incorporating a tun, or barrel, to represent the second syllable, but the other half of this pictorial pun, a hare, is not so easy to explain. According to experts the 'Wat' in Watton derives from Wada, the Anglo-Saxon who founded the settlement, but apparently a 'wat' used to be the local name for a hare. Presumably some-one said. 'There goes a hare,' someone else cried 'There goes a what?' - and the name stuck. Anyway that accounts for the one leaping over the barrel.

The two chubby children lolling beneath the tree are the famous 'Babes in the Wood', looking rather more cherubic than one normally pictures them. They are said to have been murdered and then buried in nearby Wayland Wood, and legend has it that their cries can still be heard, though sceptics say it is just seagulls.

The Babes also feature on the sign at nearby Griston, since they are believed to have lived at Griston Hall. On that sign they are portrayed, not as cherubs, but as Tudor teen-agers. Pantomime Babes seem to come somewhere in between.

WEASENHAM

It is not simple to agree on the design and location of a sign in a village that is divided into two parishes, each with its own parish council, its own church, its own pub - and its own ideas about village signs. So all credit for devising one which has satisfied everybody. The centrepiece is the village pond, flanked by the churches of St Peter and All Saints, and the two pubs are represented by an ostrich and a fox and hounds.

The Ostrich Inn, together with much of the village, was part of the Earl of Leicester's estate, and this unlikely bird is on the family coat of arms. The fox and hounds also have an extra significance; the West Norfolk Hunt used to have their kennels in Weasenham until the 1950s. The pigeons with a crown on the sign recall another recent feature of the village; the royal racing pigeons were looked after by Mr Alan Pearce at his cottage on the green for seven years until his death in 1991. Finally the sheep recall a former annual sheep fair.

The sign is tactfully sited on the line of dots on the map that divides the two parishes - which gives a new meaning to the phrase, 'sign on the dotted line'....

WEREHAM

Wereham is a picture-book village clustered around its duck-pond and its church, and, standing between the two, it has at first glance a picture-book sign. There indeed is the church and its patron saint, St Margaret, and there is also the pond, showing the conduit which was installed by it in 1850. But the duck-pond does not just have ducks. Rising form the water is the unlikely figure of a seal.

The story of Billy the Seal is quite fascinating, not least because it is true. In 1932 Mr Luddington, who lived at the Manor House near the pond, brought home a seal that had been caught in the Wash off Hunstanton, and installed it in the pond. It soon became a village favourite, turning up on people's doorsteps for food and visiting the pub across the road for its regular pint.

Alas, after two years of rural bliss, Billy died. Some say he was hit by a car on the way to the pub, others that he got tar on his stomach from the road and it gave him a fatal infection. But however he died, Billy has now achieved immortality on the village sign.

Wereham is the setting for *The Boy at Willows End* by Frank Wrigley

WEST DEREHAM

West Dereham's most famous son was the versatile Hubert Walter, who in the thirteenth century managed to combine the offices of Lord Chief Justice, Lord Chancellor and Archbishop of Canterbury, and in his spare time founded a monastery where Abbey Farm now stands. It all seems to qualify him for a place of honour on the village sign. Certainly it bears two medieval shields, but the central character is a humble chap in a flat cap, smoking a pipe and driving a horse and cart containing what looks uncommonly like manure.

That indeed is what it is, but of a very uncommon kind. It is a load of coprolite, which sounds like a cross between a new kind of plastic and a butter substitute, but is actually defined as 'rounded stony modules which are the fossilised faeces of Palaeozoic, Mesozoic and Tertiary animals' - known locally as dinosaur dung. But experts tell me the variety found at West Dereham was more probably shark's dung, from the period when Norfolk was under water and sharks were a lot bigger than they art today. When the tide eventually went out, it left behind deposits of the stuff, which the shrewd folk of West Dereham dug up and sold to a fertiliser factory in Ipswich.

So full marks to West Dereham for originality - and Hubert Walter, eat your heart out!

WEST RUNTON

When the old wooden sign collapsed – by a happy chance, just before the Millennium – the Women's Institute, which erected it for the Queen's silver jubilee, suggested that local schoolchildren might compete to provide a new design. Twelve-year-old Chantell Smith produced one which combined some of the traditional features of Harry Carter's original with a dramatic new addition, and West Runton must have the only sign in Norfolk that stars a mammoth. Not a mammoth something, just a mammoth...

It is depicted in front of the cliffs where its bones were recently uncovered, a reminder of a prehistoric age. The shepherd's crook on the post, all that remains of the old sign, and the flock of sheep recall more recent days of free grazing on common land, and the horse, the rowing boat, the campers and the golfers bring it all right up to date. The horse has a special significance in this village, which is the home of the Norfolk Shire Horse Centre.

There was a final happy touch to link the old sign with the new. The veteran singer and broadcaster Ian Wallace, who has a holiday home here, repeated his unveiling ceremony of twenty-seven years before.

WESTWICK

When the elegant Westwick arch, which used to span the main road, was demolished in 1981, the villagers were so sad to lose their celebrated landmark that they set up a fund to commemorate it. Photographs of the original arch were sold to help raise money, people volunteered their services and gave materials, and the village sign, with its accurate replica of the arch, is the result.

The sign also features the eighteenth-century obelisk, another noted landmark. It still stands, but it has lost its iron roof and the observatory at the top, and the entrance has been blocked because the steps became too dangerous. According to local people it was built after two sisters married the squires of Westwick and adjoining Worstead. The sisters fell out and the Westwick squire erected it on his land so he and his wife could watch everything happening in his neighbour's domain. This, of course, was before the invention of planning regulations...

There are also cherries here, a reminder of the cherry orchards, which provided a sea of blossom in the springtime, and inevitably a sheep, an essential part of the landscape when the Worstead weavers were close by.

WINFARTHING

Winfarthing used to be set in a thousand-acre deer forest, and there are two reminders of it on the sign, a deer and the 'ER I'. The first Queen Elizabeth granted local men exemption from jury duty so that they could guard the forest. The sign also marks the present queen's silver jubilee, hence the matching 'ER II'.

The plough, the church, the stocks and the loaves of Easter charity bread surround a modest-sized oak which in reality was some forty feet in circumference and one of the oldest in England. It finally blew down about fifty years ago.

On the post is the Good Sword of Winfarthing, which also features in a stained-glass window in the church. Legend says a thief was given sanctuary and left it behind in gratitude. It had a curious combination of powers: it located lost horses and disposed of unwanted husbands. Their lives could be shortened 'if that the wife who was weary of her husband would set a candle before that sword every Sunday for the space of a year, no Sunday excepted'. If the wife was in a hurry I suppose the sword itself might offer a speedier solution. Either way, nervous husbands will be glad to know the sword has long since gone.

WINTERTON

The ploughman and the drifter on the sign could represent almost any village on the Norfolk coast, but at Winterton the seascape has a special significance. Many seafarers have come to grief in these waters, including Daniel Defoe's accident-prone hero Robinson Crusoe. Defoe knew this coast well – 'one of the most dangerous and most fatal to sailors in all England', he wrote – and he chose this setting for Crusoe's first shipwreck. He described how Crusoe's ship was caught in a storm and those on board had to be rescued and rowed ashore 'past the lighthouse at Winterton' – which features on the sign.

Crusoe was apparently fit enough to walk the five or six miles to Yarmouth to get transport back to London. The next time he was wrecked he found himself in more exotic surroundings but with nowhere to walk to, and just his man Friday for company – but at least he survived on both occasions. There are many graves of less fortunate shipwreck victims in Winterton churchyard, and the church has a Fisherman's Corner in memory of local fatalities, created by a Rector who subsequently died himself while rescuing a drowning choirboy.

WOLFERTON

The sign, erected by George V on the Royal Estate, illustrates the ancient Norse morality tale of Fenrir the demon wolf and Tyr the god of war. The gods found Fenrir and tried to tame him, but the bigger he grew - and he did grow very big - the more savage he became. Then they tried to trick him, by putting chains round him on the pretext of testing his strength. He duly tested it, and broke the chains. So they got a magician to produce an unbreakable silken thread, and suggested Fenrir tried his strength on that. He agreed, if one of the gods would put his hand between his jaws. Tyr nobly agreed, and Fenrir was tied up. This time he could not get free, but bit off Tyr's hand.

The moral is that evil cannot be appeased, it can only be conquered by faith and self-sacrifice. Oddly enough, according to the experts, the Wolf in Wolferton has nothing to do with wolves, demon or otherwise; it is not even of Norse origin. The name comes from *Wylfhere-tun*, meaning Wylfhere's settlement. Wylfhere could just be an early version of Wilfred. But never mind; it's a great story - and a jolly nice sign.

WOODRISING

Should the village's name be divided into two words? Opinion is, well, divided, but it is one word on the sign so I will do the same.

There was also the choice of some notable Lords of the Manor to put on it. Sir Francis Crane, for instance, became Chancellor of the Order of the Garter, which sounds rather grand, and won a more down-to-earth place in history by introducing tapestry-making into England. In doing so he benefited from an early form of start-up subsidy; James I gave him two thousand pounds to set up a factory at Mortlake.

His products proved popular among the Great and the Good, some of whom, as was their wont, gave him perks instead of cash. In lieu of one payment, for instance, he was granted the right to coin fifty per cent of the nation's farthings. I hope he produced enough of them to cover the bill.

Harry Carter, however, was unimpressed and chose another local squire for the sign, Sir Robert Southwell and his wife. He too rose to high office, but kept out of 'trade' and so missed out on the subsidies and the farthings.

The tower shown on the parish church fell down many years ago. There is now a quaint little thatched bell-house in the churchyard.

WOODTON

The decorations on the arms of this unusual sign, shaped rather like a weather-vane, represent the two major influences on village life, the church and agriculture, and two notable characters with Woodton connections, Lord Nelson and Woodton's answer to John Peel, a huntsman called Ned Baldry.

When the Revd Maurice Suckling, member of an ancient Woodton family, was Rector here, his daughter Catherine married another Norfolk parson called Nelson. Their son, Horatio, used to like visiting his grandfather and climbing the cedar tree portrayed on the sign, which is still known as Nelson's Tree.

Ned Baldry, chief huntsman to the squire, Robert Suckling, became so renowned for his skill he was invited all over the country and abroad to give demonstrations with his pack. His gravestone tells his story:

> *Few of his calling with him compare*
> *For skill in hunting fox or fallow deer.*
> *He shewed his art in England, Ireland, France,*
> *And rests in this churchyard, being his last Chance.*

WRETHAM

The name covers East and West Wretham, but West Wretham is not on many maps and rarely gets a mention in a gazetteer. Lady Harrod's Norfolk Guide does note briefly that the Hall was burnt down in 1906, the rebuilt version was later demolished and the church is a ruin. 'Obviously not a lucky village,' she comments, and perhaps that is reflected by one unusual feature on the sign.

Much of the design is familiar, the Breckland countryside with some partridges relaxing before the shooting season begins. There is also a ram's head, recalling the custom of releasing a ram and allowing it to be kept by whoever caught it. The ram was provided by Eton College, the main local landlord; the origin of the tradition is probably as obscure as the rules of the Eton wall-game.

But the oddest feature is a witch on her broomstick, flying purposefully across the sky. There are many local tales of witchcraft, but perhaps her sinister presence is mainly connected with West Wretham, 'obviously not a lucky village'. She may be the reason why.

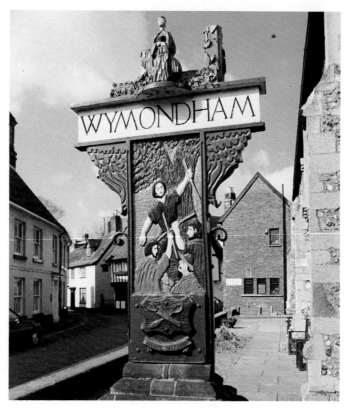

WYMONDHAM

When an emblem is needed to represent Wymondham, it generally gets the wooden spoon; not because it is worse than anywhere else, but because it used to have a famous wood-turning industry which produced that sort of thing. So there is a wooden spoon and a spigot on the sign, together with a turner at work.

On the other side is Robert Kett, leader of the 1549 rebellion against the enclosure of common lands. He is rallying his followers under Kett's Oak, which still stands on their route from Wymondham to Norwich. He had more than three, of course, but they still lost the rebellion and Kett was hanged at Norwich Castle. However, he is still a local hero.

On top of the sign is a Benedictine monk outside Wymondham Abbey with its two towers. He may be standing guard, because the townspeople had a long and bitter feud with the monks over the towers and who had the right to hang bells in them. They even petitioned Henry IV to sort things out. One way and another, in fact, Wymondham folk used to cause quite a stir. Maybe that is the real reason for the wooden spoon...